P9-BZB-898

Presented
to my friend

with love
from

Look on pages 5, 26, 55 and 56 for additional places to add your friend's name!

Katrina ❀ Alexis ❀ Korrine ❀ Melanie

Jenny ❀ Dorothea ❀ Monica ❀ Pam

Lori ❀ Gina ❀ Nona ❀ Debbie ❀ Staci

Pat ❤ Margie ❤ Ruth ❤ Sharon

Katherine ❤ Elizabeth ❤ Vicki ❤ Kathy ❤ Peggy ❤ MaryBeth

Chris ❤ Laurie ❤ Gail ❤ Marsha ❤ Michelle ❤ Liz ❤ Janice ❤ Georgene

Cindy ❤ Beth ❤ Sue ❤ Angel ❤ Nancy ❤ Connie ❤ Sandi ❤ Dianne ❤ Valoy ❤ Barbara ❤ Marianne

Althea ❤ Darlene ❤ Sherry ❤ Carol

DEDICATED
to
MY GIRLFRIENDS

past, present, and future ♥

Amy ❀ Charlene ❀ Carmen ❀ Karen

2

The Blessing of Friendship

A Gift from the Heart

KARLA DORNACHER

COUNTRYMAN

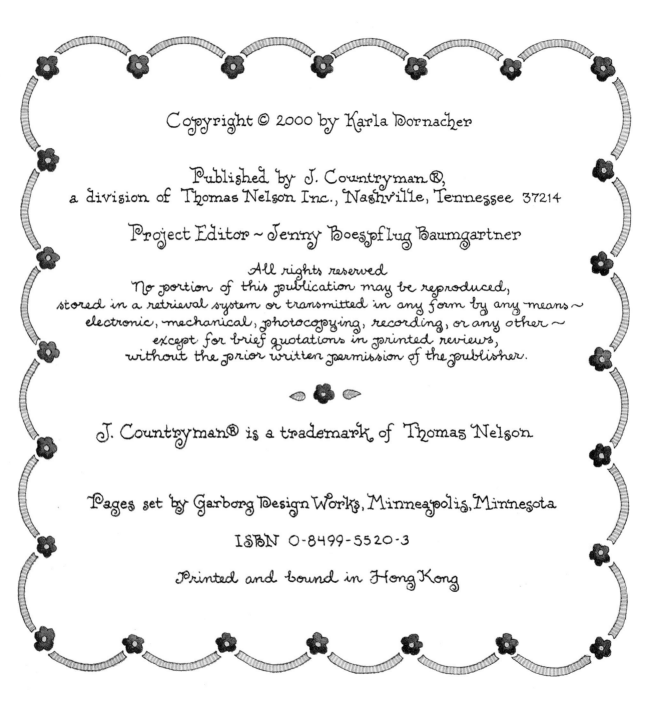

BLESS ♥ YOU!

Most of us are familiar with this little phrase, which is spoken, sometimes even by a total stranger, upon the release of a sneeze. But there's more to a blessing than just words. A blessing is like a beautifully wrapped present waiting to be opened and enjoyed. It is a gift filled with love, good tidings, and promise.

The friendship of other women is one such blessing! It comes to us as a gift from God, the best blessing-giver of all, and it is wrapped and ribboned in the heart and life, tears and laughter, and caring and sharing of someone we would call a true friend.

The Bible tells us of another friendship blessing ~ the greatest of all of God's gifts ~ His Son Jesus. No truer Friend will ever be found.

I hope that as you read the words and delight in the illustrations of this little book, you will be moved to celebrate the gift and blessing of friendship, both with Jesus and with other women.

Bless you,
Karla

be encouraged in heart

and united in love. COLOSSIANS 2:2

7

Have you ever tried to find
the "perfect" gift to give a special friend?
You want her to know how much you care,
so you are willing to shop 'til you drop to find it!

To give the perfect gift
you must first know the heart of your friend.
It needs to fit who she is . . .
her personality, her style, her season of life!

Because God already knows your heart,
your friends are His perfect gift to you.
He knows the need for a proper fit!
Consider for a moment the friendships you've enjoyed.
Every one has been unique, no two alike.
Each one was chosen with great care, by God, especially for you!

We may sometimes even wonder at God's choice,
but He knows us and our needs better than we know ourselves.
He gives us friends, not only for our own blessing,
but to teach us to be better blessing~givers.

May we rejoice in the goodness
of the greatest Gift~Giver of all
and in the gifts of friendship we've been given.

Every good and every perfect gift is from above.

James 1:17 NKJV

Hand in hand, we

heart to heart.

walk together,

friends forever.

My husband and I live in the Great Northwest,
and we love it here. Though the climate is mild,
we have more than our share of rainy days.
For many, this lack of sunlight can be depressing,
but when the skies turn blue and the sun decides to shine,
folks begin to smile, and joy fills the air.
There is a sense of celebration everywhere you go!

Jesus is called the "light of the world."
Walk with Him as your closest Friend,
and you cannot help but soak up
the glorious streams of His love and blessing.
As the light of His goodness flows
into the dark and dreary places of your heart,
despair gives way to hope, and there truly is a sense of
celebration and joy in His presence!

God calls us "children of light."
As we walk through life, we are like stars in the darkness,
shining God's love and blessing into the lives of those around us.
The more we reflect the character of the Son,
the brighter we shine.
It is the warm rays of love, generosity,
integrity, honesty, and caring
that bring life to the heart of true friendship.

Walk as children of light

in all goodness, righteousness, and truth.

EPHESIANS 5:8 NKJV

You brighten my day

You light up my life

You warm my heart

This little light
of mine,
I'm going to
let it shine!

My cup
runneth
over

Psalm 23:15 NKJV

Even though I am a coffee~by~choice woman,
I delight in a hot cup of tea served in a beautiful floral teacup
and savored in the company of dear friends.

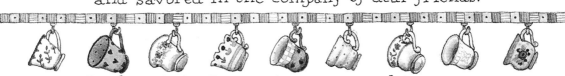

My friend Sandi collects teacups and teapots ~
not just because they are so pretty,
but because she truly enjoys tea, much like I enjoy my coffee.
Whenever I visit her, she always has the teakettle whistling,
ready to fill my cup with some fragrant herbal brew.
This friend graciously serves me not only a cup of tea,
but also the cup of total acceptance and love ~
a drink of blessing that overflows my heart.

I first met Sandi during a very difficult time of my life.
I was emotionally wounded and lonely.
She somehow saw through the "bandages" I had applied to my heart,
not bandages for healing, but for protection.
She reached out with the love of Christ and encouraged me
as I loosened the thick wrappings and allowed myself
to once again experience the true friendship of other women.

Dear Jesus, help me to have a servant's heart ~
to be a woman who pours a drink more refreshing than tea.
May the cup I offer to the women you have placed in my life
always overflow with your love and acceptance.

Remember a time when
a friend poured out her love
and warmed your heart.

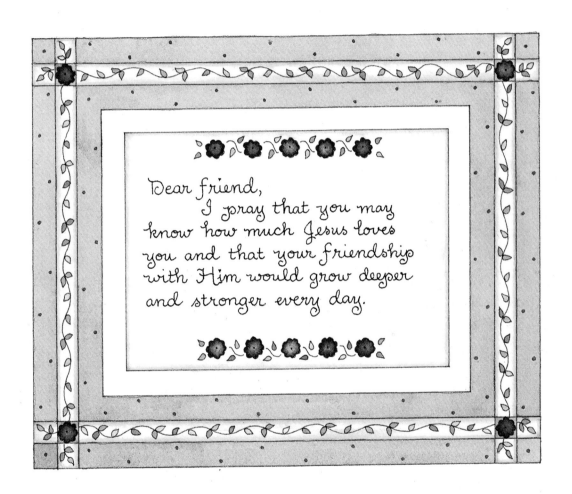

Dear friend,
    I pray that you may know how much Jesus loves you and that your friendship with Him would grow deeper and stronger every day.

"Oh Peggy, I can't do this!" I sobbed, as I anxiously poured out my heart over the telephone from two thousand miles away. I was supposed to speak before a group of people in less than an hour, and fear had overcome me. All I could do was cry!

I thank God for praying friends like Peggy!
When I call her, I am confident that she will not feel sorry for me
or try to "fix" me but she will lead me to Jesus,
the only One who can truly meet my needs.

We all have struggles in life,
moments when we want to run and hide,
fears that overcome us,
circumstances we don't know how to handle.
I know how difficult it can be to share these struggles with others,
to be vulnerable and express our need or sin or failure.
But we need to look for and be the kind of friend Peggy is,
one who will use times of weakness to point us to Jesus.

A power is released into our lives through prayer,
one that is not available through any other activity on earth.
It is a power that breaks down walls, unites our hearts,
and leads us to look to and depend on Jesus and not ourselves.

In everything by prayer and supplication

with thanksgiving,
let your requests be made known to God.

Philippians 4:6 NKJV

Scatter seeds of blessing wherever you go . . .

and watch your garden
of friendship grow!

Friends are flowers in the garden of life.

SEEDS

FRIENDSHIP GARDEN

26

FRIENDSHIP GARDEN

Welcome

The tending of a friendship garden is no small matter
and not to be taken lightly.
Many a beautiful garden has gone to ruin for lack of proper care.
Here are some tips that may prove helpful:

Heart~Soil Preparation

Prepare the soil by tilling it with God's unconditional love.
Remove any rocks of judgement or critical attitudes.
Pull out any roots of fear and jealousy.
Destroy the seeds of gossip before they can even take root.

Seedtime

Seeds of friendship may be found most anywhere.
Plant with care, using kind words and a listening ear.
Germination is usually spontaneous, so be watchful.
To ensure growth, water with kind deeds and a generous heart.

Maintenance

Make sure you give each friend plenty of room to grow.
Be realistic … don't expect a marigold to smell like a rose.
Fertilize generously with laughter and joy.
Water deeply with tears of empathy and prayer to
develop healthy roots and a stronger, more stable friendship.

Cultivating a friendship garden requires
patience, perseverance, and time…
but it's worth it!

Do you remember when . . .?
We all have important events, answered prayers, and precious
moments that can easily get lost in the blur of everyday busyness ~
lost and sometimes, sadly, gone forever!
The memories of these special times are important reminders of
God's love and goodness in our lives, and they need to be
recorded for His glory and our encouragement.

I have a collection of friendship memorabilia ~
cards, letters, photos, birth announcements, ticket stubs, and more.
From the laughter shared at a retreat
to the tears shed when we moved away,
many treasured memories are marked with a memento.

We all have the opportunity to capture and preserve memories,
not only for ourselves but as gifts of love for our friends.
I once had a lot of fun creating a small scrapbook album
for my friend Katherine.
A remembrance of her baby shower held in my backyard,
it was a gift from my heart and hands that she could
treasure long after her son had outgrown his diapers!

Take a walk down memory lane.
As you pause along the path to enjoy those special moments
from days gone by, take time to thank God for each blessing
and ask Him how you might give
the gift of a memory to a special friend.

The memory of the righteous will be a blessing.

PROVERBS 10:7 NIV

Dear Friend,
I am so thankful for our friendship! Whether near or faraway!
Love you

PHOTOS

Here are some suggestions for capturing and preserving memories

EVENTS YOU MAY WANT TO REMEMBER

birthday   marriage   anniversary

wedding or baby shower

retreat   housewarming party   baptism

a musical, play, or conference you attended together

THINGS YOU MAY WANT TO COLLECT

photos of everything ~ people, places, food, anything fun

wrapping paper and ribbon from gifts

flowers to dry   ticket stubs   programs

napkins   postcards   maps

before you go, remind yourself to be on the lookout for these

PROJECTS YOU MAY WANT TO MAKE

a small photo album or just a couple of pages for an album

a fabric~covered foamboard with mementos tucked inside

a framed invitation or photo

(inscribe a brass plate to commemorate the moment and tack it to the frame!)

buy a promise book for the occasion
and ask a number of friends to write notes in it

Create a memory page for yourself or a friend.

Remember when. . .

Giggle, laugh, and make joyful noises!

God gave us such a wonderful gift
when He gave us the capacity to laugh!
And how much greater is that gift when shared with a friend.
The Bible encourages us to develop a cheerful heart,
not only for our own well-being,
but also for encouraging and uplifting others.

My friend Fern calls me once in a while
to ask if I have anything to donate to a charity organization.
Whether I say "yes" or "no," she always makes me chuckle
by sharing a simple silly joke.
She is a friend who cultivates humor and reaps a smile
from me every time.

I want to be that kind of friend, don't you?

Struggles and challenges will always be a part of life,
but they don't have to consume us.
Jesus came to give us abundant life,
and He wants us to enjoy it.
Take time to play, to be silly, to have fun!
Cut out a comic. Write down a joke.
Look for humor in the everyday "stuff" and share it with a friend!

He will yet fill your mouth with laughter and your lips with shouts of joy.

JOB 8:21 NIV

Dear Friend,

Why is the letter A
like a flower?

Because a bee comes
after it!

Just a funny to make you smile!
Hugs....Karla

Why do bees hum?

Because they don't know the words!

1 - 2 - - 3
4 - - 5 - - 6

Why is six afraid of seven?

Because seven eight nine!

What starts with T,
ends with T,
and is full of T ?

A teapot!

Journal a memory of when a friend made you giggle . . . or tickle a friend with a silly story of your own.

Above all things put on love

Adapted from Colossians 3:14 NKJV

Did you ever play "dress up" when you were a little girl?
A friend once told me that she and her girlfriends
took themselves very seriously as they
wiggled into her mom's old dresses and high-heeled shoes.

As adults, we need to be aware that we can still help
"dress" each other in godly garments
by the way we relate and interact as friends.

The Bible says we are to put on
"the garment of praise for the spirit of heaviness" (ISAIAH 61:3).
When you call a friend who you know is struggling
and help her find joy in the midst of her trying circumstances,
you are showing her how to put on that garment of praise.
When you confide in a friend and ask her to pray for you,
you're giving her the opportunity to put on love and compassion
and reflect the character of Christ.

But we must be careful:
we can pick up and put on filthy rags by mistake.
Gossip, grumbling, covetousness, and complaining
are not pretty, and they can feel uncomfortable and heavy.

So get serious: call your girlfriends
and help them wiggle into some of God's glorious garments.

Follow the leader!
It's a game most of us know from our childhood.
The leader would feel so special ~
hopping and skipping and twirling around ~
while the rest of us, the followers, would giggle and laugh,
trying to imitate her every move.

When I first met Sandi, she was the new leader of the women's ministry,
and I was new in the church.
As I watched her, I knew she was a woman I wanted to imitate.
In fact, I met several women that year
who not only became my good friends
but also greatly influenced my life as they led me, by their example,
into a deeper love for the Lord, His Word, and His people.

Whether we realize it or not, we are all leaders. . . and followers!
We are all in a position
to influence and be influenced by those around us.
I thank God for those friends who have had such a godly influence
on my life, and I pray that I might be that kind of friend to others.

We are called to be like Jesus,
to live a life characterized by humility and unconditional love;
to serve, not be served;
and to love God and people more than things or experiences.

Follow Jesus and let love lead!

Follow the way of love.

1 Corinthians 14:1 NIV

We all have moments when we feel insignificant and alone.
Maybe you're feeling that way right now.
Everywhere you look, other people are busy with their own lives.
They don't seem to even see you.
You want to reach out, but your cup is empty.
And you feel as though you have nothing to offer.

Dear friend, we can become so discouraged when we're alone.
The more we look to others, the more parched and empty
we can become until we think we might die of thirst.
We can choose to be hurt or angry.
We can even try to fill our own cup.
But being alone may very well
be God's design to draw you closer to Himself.
He longs to be your very best friend.
He loves you more than you'll ever comprehend,
and He alone is able to meet the deepest needs of your heart.

As you make Jesus the center of your life,
He fills your emptiness to overflowing,
with plenty left over to share.

When you reach out with this cool, refreshing drink of God's love ~
one of acceptance, compassion, mercy, and encouragement ~
you may soon find another drinking from the same cup,
and you both will be refreshed.

She who refreshes others will herself be refreshed.

adapted from Proverbs 11:25 NIV

There are many ways of refreshing others.
Here are just a few~

smile

offer a listening ear

send her a Bible verse

take a walk in the park together

write a note of thanks

share a cup of tea

give her a plate of cookies

invite her to a movie

send her a bouquet of flowers

share a favorite recipe

give her a gift for no reason

pray

weed her garden

call her on the phone

offer to watch her kids

buy her a bottle of bubble bath

remember her birthday

laugh

go for ice cream together

invite her to lunch

Two are better than one, because they have a good return for their work.

Ecclesiastes 4:9 NIV

A cord of three strands is not quickly broken.

Encouragement

Joy

Trust

Ecclesiastes 4:12 NIV

Thank you for being a true and faithful friend.

Write a note of thanks to a friend who prayed with you during a difficult time.

Have you ever disappointed a friend? Not lived up to her expectations?
I have. In fact, I've lost friends because they were not able
to forgive my shortcomings or, in some cases, accept me for who I am.

I remember the first time I disappointed my friend Kathy.
I had forgotten to do something I said I would do,
and even though it was unintentional, she had every right to be upset.
But instead of being angry, she said with a smile,
"It's okay. I give you grace."
Hearing those words was like sweet music to my ears.
I was forgiven and accepted . . . even though I had failed!

Grace is unmerited favor. It is God's gift
of unconditional love, forgiveness, and acceptance ~
even when we don't deserve it!
Like Kathy, when we accept this gift from God through faith in Jesus,
we are able to share it with others.

Have any of your friends ever failed or disappointed you?
Showed up late? Forgotten your birthday? Hurt your feelings?
If they haven't . . . they will!
We are all imperfect people, and we all make mistakes.
We all need grace!

There is only one Friend who will never fail you
and that's Jesus.
For all your other friends . . . give them grace!

God makes all things beautiful in His time.

Adapted from Ecclesiastes 3:11 NIV

50

We all seem to struggle with not having enough time!
How do we ever find time to enjoy and invest in our friendships?
My friends and I are so thankful for our telephone visits,
but we still need face to face encounters ~ complete with hugs.

The most important investment of your time
needs to be with your Best Friend.
Jesus should be the first one to whom you run
when you have a problem,
and the first one with whom you celebrate blessings!
I have found that when I spend time with Him in the morning,
He has a way of fitting in all that I need during the day,
including other friends.

Take a moment to look at your busy schedule.
What do you normally do by yourself that you might be able to do
with a friend? In days gone by, women got together for quilting bees,
canning, and food preserving. Surely there's something in your life
that can be done in the company of other women.

Bible studies and prayer groups offer a chance
to grow spiritually as well as connect with like-minded women.
Walking with friends combines physical exercise
with inspiration and encouragement.
Why not get together and mend socks, sew quilts for the homeless,
read to one another, or even go shopping?
Look in your life for opportunities to connect with other women ~
and then do it!

XOXOXO

What activities have you enjoyed with a friend?

God is the greatest **Gift-Giver** of all!
He gives us food to eat and water to drink and offers
us unconditional love, comfort, encouragement, and wisdom.
Most of all, He gives us the gift of eternal life through
His only Son, Jesus Christ.

Have you accepted God's gift of salvation?
Have you received any encouragement from His Word?
Have you found peace or comfort or joy in His love?

to you
from God

Freely you have received;
freely you are asked to give.

The Bible says a generous person will prosper and be blessed!
If you desire friendships that will bless your life,
then be a friend who gives herself away generously!

Be willing to listen when your friend is burdened.
Offer to make meals or clean the house for a friend in need.
Write notes of encouragement to a working friend who needs a lift.
Baby~sit for a friend so she can use the free time as she chooses.
Send a handmade gift or craft as an anonymous gift of blessing.
Take her flowers for absolutely no reason at all!
And the list goes on . . .

Whatever you give,
give it generously as unto the Lord,
and give it with a smile!

God loves a cheerful giver.

The Holy Bible

To my friend-

God's Promises

Oil of Love

Memories

Love

2 CORINTHIANS 9:7 NKJV

It is more blessed to give than to receive

Acts 20:35 NKJV

Thank you
for giving so much to me,

Rejoice with those who rejoice

Romans 12:15 NKJV

58

It can be hard when you've wanted something for so long
only to see a friend receive the blessing instead of you.
Maybe it's a new house, a promotion, or a position of leadership
in the church. Even worse, it might be when your friends get married
and you're still single or have babies and you're still barren.
Your thoughts and emotions naturally become confused.
You love your friend,
but why is God choosing to bless her and not you?

As difficult as it may be at times,
God asks us to rejoice with those who rejoice ~
without being jealous or bitter.
God desires us to trust Him even when we don't understand.
When we are confident in His perfect plan for our lives,
we will want the best for our friends as well.

I have experienced the pain from both perspectives.
But I also know the joy and peace that comes
when you are able to trust God and rejoice in His goodness ~
even when it's not happening to you!

When something good happens in our lives,
we want a friend who can truly feel glad with us . . .
let's choose to be that kind of friend.

Weep with those who weep

Romans 12:15 NKJV

I have a friend who endured a terrible loss.
Her grief clung to her like a heavy shawl around her shoulders.
I could not take the shawl from her,
but I could come alongside her and lift a corner of that shawl
upon myself to help her bear its weight.
More than once she apologized for being a burden,
but I assured her ~ that's what friends are for.

It's not always easy, at least for me,
to develop the ability to listen and embrace
without offering advice or correction
and without sharing my own equally traumatic experiences.
And I must confess that there were moments
when I wanted her to put it behind her.
I yearned for days to come
when we would share more joy than sorrow.
But grief must be walked out, step by tearful step.

The Bible tells us that we are not to grow weary in doing good
because joy returns to those who wait patiently on the Lord!
Never quit praying and never give up . . .
on your friend or your God!

There is a time to speak, to embrace, and to encourage.
And there is a time to quietly come alongside,
lift the shawl, and be a friend.

Write about a time when a friend
loved you in a special way ~
in rejoicing or weeping.

_____

_____

_____

_____

_____

_____

_____

_____

_____

_____

_____

_____

_____

good times

crying times

happy times

bad times

laughing times

sad times

A friend loves at all times

12
11
10
9
8
7
6
5
4
3
2
1

Proverbs 17:17 NKJV

giving times

all times!

feast times

receiving times

famine times

63

We all want so much to be loved and accepted.
The fear of rejection, of not measuring up, can sometimes cause us
to try to be something or someone we're not, just so we can fit in.
Or it can cause us to never risk entering into a relationship at all.

What a friend you have in Jesus!
You don't ever have to be afraid
of Him leaving or rejecting you.
He knows everything there is to know about you ~
He knows you're not perfect ~
and He still loves you and accepts you for who you are!

The more we are able to grasp this truth,
to find our value and security in Jesus alone,
the more able we are to accept ourselves and others.
God's love sets us free to be who He designed us to be.
It also releases us from the fear of rejection
and the need to live up to someone else's expectations.

Jesus is our example of a perfect friend.
His perfect love is our standard.

We are called to love our friends as Jesus loves us.
They need to be free to be all God designed them to be,
and to know they are loved . . . even when they're not perfect!

"Love one another as I have loved you."
~ Jesus

John 15:12 NKJV

65

The
heartfelt counsel
of a friend
is as sweet as
perfume.

Proverbs 27:9 NLT

The Bible spares no ink
in teaching and warning us of the power of our words!

We are told that words hold the potential for life and death!
They have the ability to lift a spirit, transform an attitude,
instill hope, and alter eternity!
Thoughtlessly said, they can also wound the heart 💜,
destroy a vision, instill fear, and distort the truth!

We need to have friends and be friends
who will speak wisely.

Our conversations should always be to build up and encourage,
never to tear down.
Our counsel should always be preceded by prayer
and showered with grace
Our commitment should always be to speak the truth
with love and integrity.

And remember that Jesus is your ever~present friend,
the unseen guest in every conversation.
May the fragrance of your words be pleasing to Him
and a blessing to all.

You always listen
when I need an ear,
you comfort my heart
and wipe my tear,
your counsel is godly,
full of wisdom, and true,
I thank God for
giving me
a friend like
you.

Your friendship

blesses my heart

A friend once said,
"You can't really know me until you've been in my home."
There is some truth to this statement.

We meet and enjoy each other in a variety of places ~
church, community meetings, our place of business, or school.
These are generally safe, nonthreatening environments
where we can reveal only as much about ourselves as we desire ~
places where we can keep people, even our friends, at arm's length.

God does not desire that we hold our arms out in front of us
to keep people at a distance,
but that we hold them wide open
to invite people into our lives and our homes.

Hospitality is not about how big your house is
or how it's decorated.
It's not about how good a cook you are
or how you set the table.

Hospitality is about opening your heart ♥ and your home
and sharing what God has given you.
It's about being vulnerable to let others know who you are!
It's about giving yourself to someone else,
to let them know you care about them.

So put on the soup or fix some sandwiches.
Pick up the phone and invite a friend!

When God's children
are in need,
be the one to help them out.
Get into the habit
of inviting guests for dinner
or, if they need lodging,
for the night.

Romans 12:13 NLT

Use this space to remember a time
when a friend opened her heart and her home
and blessed you with hospitality.

_____

_____

_____

_____

_____

_____

_____

_____

_____

_____

_____

_____

Marsha told me
that she knew me before we even met.
But how could that be? We live thousands of miles apart.
She said she "knew me" through some magnets
she bought at a store in Texas.
Who would have imagined that God had gone before us,
to prepare the soil of our friendship,
by sending my artwork to Texas
and placing a magnet in Marsha's life?

But that is the way it is with God and friendships.
He goes before us to prepare the soil of our hearts ~
not only for our friendships with other women,
but also for friendship with Himself.
God knew you before you were even born and like that magnet,
He sends you His love ♥ and draws you to Himself
through the circumstances of your life.

For various reasons,
our friendships with others may not survive the years,
but once you meet Jesus and call Him Friend,
there is nothing that can separate you
from His powerful, magnificent, magnetic love!

You and Jesus . . . . Forever Friends!

Through my artwork and books, I have met many women and enjoyed many new friendships across the country.
In fact, the way I figure,
if you are reading and enjoying this little book, we are friends.
Maybe not talk~on~the~phone, share~the~deepest~secrets~of~our~lives, come~on~over~for~coffee~type friends,
but then, we don't know what the future holds either, do we?
I do know this, though: if you are being blessed by the words of this book and you delight in the style and detail of my art,
we are connecting at a heart level.
There is a good chance that if we ever met for lunch, we could visit and laugh for hours, and maybe even share a tear for good measure.

Heart connections are often formed as we share an interest or an activity. Moms tend to naturally connect with other moms at the playground, as they homeschool, or when they attend a PTA meeting.
I have one friend who regularly gathers with a small group of women to do needlework ~ something normally done alone becomes the link that allows them to share their lives and their needs with one another. Your heart connection may be with a Bible study group, a walking partner, or a woman at work.
It's not as important where it happens, as long as it happens.

If you are presently needing heart connections, ask God to show you where to look.
He not only knows you and your needs better than you do, but He also knows of another woman who is praying for someone to call a friend ~ and it might just be you!

F R I E N D

I need friends! You need friends! We all need friends!

We are created in the image of God to be like Him,
and He is a God of intimate relationship.
Many times, Jesus refers to His believers as His friends.
If you have placed your faith in Him,
believing that He died on the cross for your sins,
He is your Friend...and you are His!

If you haven't,
I invite you to ask Him into your heart right now.
He's calling your name!

He knows you more intimately than you know yourself,
and He loves you more than you can possibly comprehend.
His promises are true, and He is always faithful to His Word.
He always watches out for you, desiring your best,
and He will never leave you, betray you, or reject you.

The better you know Him as your Friend,
the more He fills your life,
and the more you become like Him ~
a true and faithful friend,
His hands and heart to the women friends in your life.

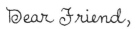

Dear Friend,

As I have written this book, I have questioned my own qualifications to do so. Friendships have not always come easy to me. Many times the offer of friendship has been accompanied by unrealistic expectations, selfish motives, and hurtful words.

My own background has been a hindrance to making friends. In the past thirty years, I have lived in ten communities and sixteen neighborhoods and know how difficult it can be to reach out and establish new relationships.

Maybe with each trial and each move, I've learned something, and with each friendship, I've grown. I must confess, I have only come to know and understand the true value of women friends since I came to know Jesus as my Best Friend. I have also come to understand that because we do live in a world filled with hurt and pain, we need more than superficial relationships. We need the love, prayers, and encouragement that only other women can give us. We need to quit being afraid of each other, afraid to reach out, to be vulnerable, to care. We need to trust Jesus and be friends. ♥

Your friend in Jesus,
Karla

There is a friend who sticks closer than a brother.
Proverbs 18:24 NKJV